Machine Learning

a Beginners Guide to the Fundamentals of Machine Learning

David Longbow

Table of Contents

CHAPTER ONE

Introduction

What is Machine Learning?

Machine learning is an artificial intelligence (AI) discipline focused on the technological development of human knowledge. Machine learning allows computers to manage new situations through analysis, self-training, observation, and experience.

Machine learning facilitates the continuous advancement of computing through exposure to new scenarios, testing, and adaptation while using trend and trend detection for improved decisions in later situations (But not identical).

Machine learning is often confused with data mining and knowledge discovery in databases (KDD), which share a similar methodology.

Other machine learning applications include syntactic pattern recognition, natural language processing, search engines, computer vision, and machine perception. It is difficult to reproduce human intuition in a machine, mainly because human beings often learn and execute decisions unconsciously.

As children, machines require a period of extended training when developing general algorithms geared towards dictating future behaviors. Training techniques include rotation learning, parameter adjustment, macro operators, sharing, explanatory learning, grouping, error correction, case registration, multiple models, retro-propagation, reinforcement learning and genetic algorithms.

Why "Learn"?

Machine-based learning involves programming computers to optimize a performance criterion by using examples of data or experience. There is no need to "learn" to calculate the wage bill. Learning is used when: human expertise does not exist (sailing on Mars), (humans are not able to explain their expertise Vocal). The solution changes on time (routing on a computer network). Solution must be adapted to particular cases (user biometry).

Machine learning studies computer algorithms to learn how to do things. For example, we might be interested in learning how to accomplish a task, making accurate predictions, or conducting ourselves intelligently. The learning that is done is always based on a kind of observations or data, such as examples (the most common case in this course), direct experience or instruction. So, in general, machine learning is about learning to do better in the future depending on what has been experienced in the past. The emphasis on machine learning is on machine methods. In other words, the goal is to design learning algorithms that all machines learn without human intervention or assistance. The learning paradigm of the machine can be considered as "programming for example." Often we have a specific task in mind, such as spam filtering. But rather than programming the computer to solve the task directly in machine learning, we are looking for methods by which the computer will offer its program according to the examples we provide. Machine learning is a central subfield of artificial intelligence. It is very unlikely that we can build any intelligent system capable of one of the facilities that we associate with intelligence, such as language or vision, without learning how to access it. These tasks are simply too difficult to solve. Moreover, we do not consider a system to be truly intelligent if it is incapable of learning because learning is at the heart of intelligence. Although it is a sub-area of AI, machine learning is also integrated into other fields, particularly statistics, but also in mathematics, physics and theoretical computing.

All except the most trivial cases, the knowledge or experience you are trying to get out of the raw data will not be obvious by looking at the data. For example, when detecting spam, searching for a single word may not be very useful. But looking at the appearance of certain words used together, combined with the length of email and other factors, you can get a much clearer picture of whether the email is spam or not. Machine learning transforms data into information.

Machine learning is at the intersection of computer science, engineering, and statistics, and often appears in other disciplines. It is a tool that can be applied to many problems. Any field that has to interpret and act on the data can benefit from machine learning techniques. Machine learning uses statistics. For most people, statistics are an esoteric topic used by companies to determine just how great their products are. (There is an excellent manual on how to call it How to Lie with Statistics by Darrell Huff.) Ironically, it is the best-selling statistics book of all time.) The practice of engineering is to apply science to solve a problem. In engineering, we are used to solving a deterministic problem where our solution solves the problem all the time. If we are asked to write software to control a distributor, it is best to work all the time, regardless of the money entered or the buttons pressed.

There are many problems where the decision is not determined. This means that we do not know enough about the problem, or we do not have enough computational power to model the problem properly. We need statistical data for these issues. For example, people's motivation is a problem that is currently too difficult to model. In social sciences, the correct 60% of the time is considered successful. If we can predict how people will behave 60% of the time, we are doing well. How can this be? Should not we have the right all the time? If we're not right all the time, doesn't it mean we're doing something wrong? For example; do people not act to increase their happiness? Can we simply predict the outcome of events involving people based on this assumption? Perhaps, but it is difficult to determine what makes everyone happy because it can vary greatly from one person to another. So even if our assumptions are true to people who increase their happiness, the definition of happiness is too complicated to model.

There are many other examples outside of human behavior that we cannot determine at present. For these issues, should we use some statistics tools to predict the outcome of events involving people based on this assumption? Perhaps, but it is difficult to determine what makes everyone happy because it can vary greatly from one person to another. So even if our assumptions are true to people who increase their happiness, the definition of happiness is too complicated to model. There are many other examples outside of human behavior that we cannot determine at present. For these issues, we need to use some statistics tools.

Examples of Machine Learning Problems

There are many examples of machine learning problems. This book will focus on classification issues where the goal is to categorize objects in a set of categories. Here are some examples:

- **Optical Character Recognition**: categorizing handwritten images with the letters represented.
- **Face Detection**: Finding faces in images (or identifying the presence of a person).
- **Filter spam**: identify email messages as spam or Spam.
- **Sharing topics**: Within a restricted domain, define the meaning of something spoken by a speaker to the extent that it can be classified into one of a set of categories.
- **Medical diagnosis**: Diagnosing a patient as a patient or non-addicted to a disease.
- **Customer segmentation**: predicting, for example, which customers will respond to a specific promotion.
- **Detecting fraud**: Identifying credit card transactions (for example) that may be Deceptive In nature.
- **Weather forecast**: let's predict whether or not to die tomorrow (in the latter case, most likely, we would most likely be more interested in assessing the probability of rain tomorrow.

In classifying, we want to categorize objects in categories. In regression, on the other hand, we try to predict real value. For example, we can predict how much it will die tomorrow. Or maybe we want to predict how much a house will sell. The scenario for richer learning is one in which the goal is to behave intelligently or make smart decisions. For example, the robot must learn to move around the environment without encountering anything. In order to use machine learning to earn money on the stock market, we can treat investments as a classification problem (whether stocks will go up or down) or a regressive problem (how much the share will increase) or release from these interim goals, we could ask the computer to learn directly how to decide to make investments to maximize wealth. The latter example is a game where the goal is to learn how to play the computer through experience.

Goals of Machine Learning

The main purpose of machine learning research is to develop general purpose algorithms of practical value. Such algorithms must be efficient. As usual, as computer scientists, we care about the efficiency of time and space. But in the context of learning, we are also very concerned about another precious resource, namely the amount of data required by the learning algorithm. Learning algorithms should also be as general as possible. We are looking for algorithms that can be easily applied to a wide range of learning problems, such as those mentioned above. Of primary importance, we want the learning outcome to be a prediction rule that is as accurate as possible in the predictions it makes. Occasionally, we may also be interested in the interpretability of the rules of prediction produced by learning. In other words, in some contexts (such as medical diagnosis), we want the computer to find rules of prediction that are easily understood by human experts.

As mentioned above, machine learning can be considered as "programming for example." What is the advantage of machine learning over direct programming? First, the results of using machine learning are often more accurate than what can be created through direct programming. The reason is that machine learning algorithms are data driven, and can examine large amounts of data. On the other hand, it is likely that a human expert is guided by inaccurate impressions or perhaps by examining a relatively small number of examples.

Also, humans often have trouble expressing what they know but have no difficulty labelling articles. For example, it is easy for all of us to label the pictures of the letters by the represented character, but we would have many problems to explain how we do it in precise terms.

Another reason to study machine learning is the hope that it will provide insights into the general phenomenon of learning. Some of the questions that could be answered include:

- What are the intrinsic properties of a particular learning problem that makes it difficult or easy to solve?
- How much do you need to know in advance about what you are learning so you can learn it effectively?
- Why are "simpler" scenarios better? This course focuses on theoretical aspects of machine learning.

The theoretical learning of the machine has many the same goals. It is expected that the theoretical study will provide insights and intuitions, if not specific algorithms, that will be useful in the design of practical algorithms. Through theory, we hope to understand the intrinsic difficulty of a given learning problem. And we also try to explain phenomena observed in real experiments with learning algorithms. This book emphasizes the study of the design and analysis of machine learning algorithms.

Growth of Machine Learning

Machine learning is preferred approach to Speech recognition, natural language processing, Computer vision, Medical outcomes analysis, Robot control, Computational biology. This trend is accelerating Improved machine learning algorithms, Improved data capture, networking, faster computers Software which are too complex to write by hand.

Machine learning techniques

Supervised learning categories and techniques Linear classifier (numerical functions)   Parametric (Probabilistic functions) Naïve Bayes, Gaussian discriminant analysis (GDA), Hidden Markov models (HMM), Probabilistic graphical models, Non-parametric (Instance-based functions) K-nearest neighbors, Kernel regression, Kernel density estimation, Local regression Non-metric (Symbolic functions) Classification and regression tree (CART), decision tree, Aggregation Bagging (bootstrap + aggregation), AdaBoost, Random forest

State of Machine Learning -Application Successes

A measure of progress in Machine Learning is its important real-world applications, such as those listed below. Although we take many of these applications for granted, it is worth noting that as early as 1985 there were almost no commercial applications of machine learning.

- **Speech recognition**. The commercial systems currently available for speech recognition use machine learning in one way or another to train the system to recognize speech. The reason is simple: the accuracy of voice recognition is greater if you train the system than if you try to program it manually. In fact, many commercial voice recognition systems involve two distinct learning phases: one before the software is sent (general system training in an independent speaker mode), and a second phase after the user buys the software (To achieve greater accuracy through training in a speaker-dependent manner).

- **Computer vision**. Many current vision systems, from face recognition systems to systems that machine all classify cell-microscope images, are developed using machine learning because the resulting systems are more accurate than hand-made programs. A large-scale application of computer vision trained using machine learning is their uses by the US Post Office to machine all classify letters containing handwritten addresses. More than 85% of handwritten mail in the United States is machine tally classified, using handwriting analysis software trained with very high accuracy, using machine learning in a very large data set.

- **Bio-surveillance**. A variety of government efforts to detect and track disease outbreaks now use machine learning. For example, the RODS project includes the real-time collection of emergency room admissions reports in western Pennsylvania and the use of machine learning software for the typical admission profile to detect abnormal patterns of symptoms and their distribution Geographical area. The current work is to add a rich set of additional data, such as retail purchases of over-the-counter drugs to increase the flow of information in the system, further increasing the need for machine learning methods given this dataset yet more complex.

- **Robot control**. Machine learning methods have been used successfully in some robot systems. For example, several researchers have demonstrated the use of machine learning to acquire control strategies for a stable helicopter flight and helicopter aerial flight aerobatics. The recent competition sponsored by Darpa, involving a robot that was driving autonomously for more than 100 miles in the desert, was won by a robot that used auto-learning to refine its ability to detect distant objects. Distance, and later seen closely).

- **Accelerate the empirical sciences**. Many data-intensive sciences now use machine learning methods to aid in the process of scientific discovery. Machine learning is being used to learn models of gene expression in the cell from high-throughput data, to discover unusual astronomical objects from massive data collected by the Sloan study and to characterize the complex patterns of brain activation that Indicate different cognitive states of Persons in fMRI scanners. Mechanical learning methods are reforming the practice of many data-intensive empirical sciences, and many of these sciences now organize workshops on auto-learning as part of their field lectures.

Importance of Machine learning

When do we need to learn the machine instead of directly programming computers to carry out the task at hand? Two aspects of a particular problem may require the use of programs that learn and improve by their "experience": the complexity of the problem and the need for adaptation. Tasks those are very complex for the program.

a) **Tasks beyond human capacity**: A wide range of functions that utilize machine learning techniques are related to the analysis of large and very complex data sets: astronomical data, conversion of medical archives into medical knowledge, weather forecasting, genomic data analysis, web search and engines, e. With more and more digital data available, it becomes clear that there are treasures of meaningful information buried in a data archive that is a very large and complex way for humans to understand. Learning to detect meaningful patterns in large and complex data sets is a promising field in which a set of programs that you learn with virtually unlimited memory capacity and accelerated processing speed of computers opens new horizons.

b) **Functions performed by animals/humans**: There are many tasks that we humans routinely perform, but our meditation on how to do them is not detailed enough to extract a well-defined program. Examples of such tasks are leadership, speech recognition, and understanding of images. In all these tasks, advanced learning programs and "learning from their experiences" programs have achieved quite satisfactory results once they have experienced enough training examples.

Adaptability, one of the limiting features of the program tools is their hardness - once the program has been written down and installed, it stays unchanged. However, many tasks change over time or from one user to another. Machine learning tools - Adaptive programs with input data - provide a solution to these issues.

By nature, they adapt to changes in the environment they interact with. Successful examples of machine learning of such problems include programs that decode handwritten text, where a fixed program can adapt to differences between handwriting for different users. Spam detection programs, machine adaptation to changes like spam, and speech recognition programs.

CHAPTER TWO

Place of Machine Learning within Computer Science

Given this sample of applications, what can we infer in general about the future role of machine learning in the field of computer applications? One way to think about this is to imagine the space of all software applications and recognize the previous applications suggest a niche within this space where machine learning has a special role to play. In particular, machine learning methods are already the best methods available for developing particular types of software, in applications where:

- The application is too complex for people to manually design the algorithm. For example, software for the tasks of basic sensor perception, such as voice recognition and computer vision, falls into this category. All of us can easily label which photographs contain an image of our mother, but none of us can jot down an algorithm to accomplish this task. Here machine learning is the software development method of choice simply because it is relatively easy to collect tagged training data, and relatively inefficient to try to write a successful algorithm.

- The application requires the software to adapt to its operating environment once it has been installed in the field. An example of this is voice recognition systems that are customized for the user who buys the software. Mechanical learning provides the mechanism of adaptation. Software applications that are customized to users grow rapidly, for example, libraries that are customized to your purchasing preferences or e-mail readers that are customized to your particular definition of spam. This machine learning niche within the software world is growing rapidly.

Seen in this way, machine learning methods play a key role in the computing world, within an important and growing niche. While there will be software applications where machine learning will never be useful (for example, to write matrix multiplication programs), the niche where it will be used grows rapidly as applications grow in complexity, as the Demand for custom software. Computers gain access to more data and as we develop increasingly effective machine learning algorithms. Beyond its obvious role as a method for software development, machine learning is also likely to help reform our view of Computer Science more generally. By changing the question of "how to program computers" to "how to allow them to be programmed," machine learning emphasizes the design of self-diagnosing and self-repair self-monitoring systems, and the approaches that model their users, and Take advantage of the constant flow of data flowing through the program rather than simply processing it. Similarly, Learning Machine will help to reshape the field of statistics, putting a computer perspective in the foreground and raising issues such as endless learning. Of course, both Computer Science and Statistics will also help shape Machine Learning as they move forward and provide new ideas to change the way we view learning.

Who's using machine learning?

Most industries that work with large amounts of data have recognized the value of machine learning technology. By extracting information from this data, often in real time, organizations can work more efficiently or gain an advantage over their competitors.

Financial services

Banks and other companies in the financial sector use machine learning technology for two key purposes:

Identifying important data on data and preventing fraud. Ideas can identify investment opportunities, or help investors know when to trade. Data mining can also identify clients with high-risk profiles, or use cyber surveillance to signal fraud warning signals.

Government

Government agencies, such as public security and utilities, have a particular need for machine learning, as they have multiple sources of data that can be extracted to obtain information. Analyzing sensor data, for example, identifies ways to increase efficiency and save money. Machine learning can also help detect fraud and minimize identity theft.

Health care

Machine learning is a rapidly growing trend in the healthcare industry, thanks to the advent of portable devices and sensors that can use data to assess a patient's health in real time. The technology can also help medical experts analyze data to identify trends or red flags that can lead to better diagnosis and treatment.

Marketing and sales

Websites that recommend items that you may like, based on previous purchases use auto-learning to analyze your purchase history and promote other items that interest you. This ability to capture data, analyze it and use it to customize a shopping experience. A marketing campaign is the future of retailing.

Oil and gas

Find new sources of energy. Analysis of minerals in the soil, predict the failure of the refinery sensor. Rationalization of the distribution of oil to make it more efficient and profitable, the number of machine learning use cases for this industry is huge and still expanding.

Transport

Analyzing data to identify patterns and trends is essential to the transportation industry, which is based on making the routes more efficient and predicting potential problems to increase profitability. Data analysis and modeling aspects of machine learning are important tools for delivery companies, public transport, and other transport organizations.

What are some popular machine learning methods?

Two of the most widely adopted machine learning methods is supervised learning and unsupervised learning; but there are also other methods of machine learning. Here is an overview of the most popular types.

Supervised learning algorithms are trained using labelled examples, such as an input where the desired output is known. For example, a piece of equipment might have data points labelled "F" (failed) or "R" (runs). The learning algorithm receives a set of inputs along with the corresponding correct outputs, and the algorithm learns by comparing its actual output to the correct outputs to find errors. Then modify the model accordingly. Through methods such as classification, regression, prediction, and gradient increase, supervised learning uses patterns to predict label values in additional non-tagged data. Supervised learning is commonly used in applications where historical data predict likely future events. For example, you can anticipate when it is likely that credit card transactions are fraudulent or that the insurance client can file a claim.

Unsupervised learning is used against data that does not have historical labels. The system does not receive the "correct answer." The algorithm must find out what it is showing. The goal is to explore the data and find some structure inside. Unsupervised learning works well in transactional data. For example, you can identify customer segments with similar attributes that can be treated similarly in marketing campaigns. Or you can find the main attributes that separate customer segments from each other. Popular techniques include maps of self-organization, mapping of nearest neighbors, k-means grouping, and decomposition of singular values. These algorithms are also used to segment text themes, recommend items, and identify outliers of data.

Semi-supervised learning is used for the same applications as supervised learning. However, it uses tagged and unlabeled data for training, usually a small amount of data tagged with a large amount of unlabeled data (because unlabeled data is less expensive and requires less effort to acquire). This type of learning can be used with methods such as classification, regression, and prediction. Semi-supervised learning is useful when the cost associated with labeling is too high to allow for a fully labeled training process. Early examples of this include identifying a person's face on a webcam.

Reinforcement learning is often used for robotics, gaming, and navigation. With reinforcement learning, the algorithm discovers through trial and error which actions produce the greatest rewards. This type of learning has three main components: The0 agent (the learner or the decision maker), the environment (everything the agent interacts with) and actions (what the agent can do). The goal is for the agent to choose actions that maximize the expected reward over a given period. The agent will reach the goal much faster by following a good policy. So the goal in reinforcement learning is to learn the best policy.

What are the differences between data mining, machine learning, and deep learning?

Although all of these methods have the same goal: to extract ideas, patterns, and relationships that can be used to make decisions, they have different approaches and abilities.

Data mining

Data mining can be considered a superset of many different methods for extracting information from the data. It could involve traditional statistical methods and machine learning. Data mining applies methods from many different areas to identify previously unknown patterns of data. This may include statistical algorithms, machine learning, text analysis, time series analysis, and other areas of analysis. Data mining also includes the study and practice of data storage and data manipulation.

Machine learning

The main difference with machine learning is that, like statistical models, the goal is to understand the structure of the data, adjust the theoretical distributions to the data that are well understood. Therefore, with statistical models, there is a theory behind the model that is mathematically demonstrated, but this requires that the data meet certain strong assumptions as well. Machine learning has been developed by the ability to use computers to investigate structure data, even if we do not have a theory of how that structure looks. The test for a machine learning model is a validation error in new data, not a theoretical test that demonstrates a null hypothesis. Because machine learning often uses an iterative approach to learning from data, learning can be easily machine. Passes are passed through the data until a robust pattern is found.

Deep learning

Deep learning combines advances in the power of computing and special types of neural networks to learn complicated patterns in large amounts of data. Deep learning techniques are presently the state of the art for identifying objects in pictures and words in sounds. Researchers now seek to apply these successes in pattern recognition to more complex tasks such as machine language translation, medical diagnostics, and many other important social and business problems.

Difficulties encountered in Machine Learning

One-shot learning: The ability to learn with fewer or fewer examples.

Effective Response Generation: The ability to generate contextual responses.

Machine learning from a repository of resources: Learning from other resources by making a graph connected sense.

Facial Identification over varying feature space: Facial recognition is not perfect even though it is a primary requirement.

Object Detection: Machine Learning cannot understand or detect images.

Attention: Systems cannot grab attention in neural networks. So, we need to build attention mechanisms in neural networks to make them better. Machine learning cannot learn by observations and listen.

CHAPTER THREE

Difference between Machine Learning Techniques

AI and ML research has been around since computers existed. Of course, they allowed for practical creation and application. This challenge has always kept pace with the hype. Programmers were not usually able to do it - and so there were many "mistakes" of AI.

From a practical point of view, AI has got underground and provided everything from expert systems to behavioral vacuuming robots such as iRobot's Roomba. The other used an 8-bit microprocessor that used a behaviour-based rule system. Similarly, e-mail spam filters have been using Bayesian statistical techniques for decades, with varying levels of success.

AI is a very large area of research, whose machine learning is only one part. The three systems studied will be systems based on rules, Bayesian and statistical algorithms, and neural networks. These are described below:

1.   Neural Networks

Artificial neural networks (ANNs) have been in place for a long time, but their high computational requirements for complex networks have limited the use and experimentation until recently of multi-core systems such as GPGPUs that provide an economic platform for variants called deep neural networks (DNNs)

Initially, neural networks were interesting as a way of copying biological neuronal networks such as the human brain. The brain is formed by neurons that are connected through the axon to synapses and dendrites on other neurons. Electrical signals from incoming signals are summarized by the neuron. The result that exceeds the threshold value sends a signal through the axon.

ANNs are built similarly, but using electronics or software. It took many neurons to perform useful functions; the human brain has 100 billion. The trick that it has something useful is the way the neurons are connected, as well as the weights associated with neurons.

The basic neural network consists of a set of hidden-layer inputs and outputs. DNN has several hidden layers. Networks can be the same logically, but the number of inputs, outputs, and hidden layers is different as well as other configuration options.

2.   Systems based on rules and decision trees

Rule-based algorithms and decision trees are the easiest to understand. Rules-based systems consist of a set of logic rules or input-based conditions. The rule starts when its conditions are met. Running rules can change internal state variables as well as call origination.

For example, a robot can have several sensor inputs that detect touch barriers as well as motion inputs. The rule can cause the robot to stop when it moves, and the obstacle sensor starts.

Rules can create conflicting actions in which a certain priority mechanism must be implemented. For example, one rule action can stop the robot, while another wants to change its direction.

A system based on rules or behavior usually moves from one country to another and applies all the rules for each state. It is not necessary to examine all the rules depending on the implementation. For example, rules can be grouped by inputs and some need to be reviewed only if input changes.

Decision trees are a structure-based system where each node in a tree has conditions that allow grading by refining as the algorithm passes through the tree. There are many popular algorithms in this area, including CART and Chi-squared machine detection interaction

3. Bayesian and statistics

The Bayes Theorem describes the likelihood of a test result based on previous knowledge of conditions that may be related to the result. This sentence is related to the probability that event A has happened with the X, $Pr(A \mid X)$ indicator of event X probability given by A, $Pr(X \mid A)$, allows correction of measurement errors if real probabilities are known. Of course, the test results come with the probability of the test.

There are several Bayesian tree-based algorithms, including Naive Byes and Bayesian Belief Network (BBN). Like differential equations, the theory can be difficult to understand, but the application is usually simple. As noted above, Bayes algorithms have been used in applications such as email spam filtering, but are not limited to this narrow application.

Bayes is just one method that uses probability and statistics. There are also regression algorithms that have been used in machine learning. Popular regression algorithms include least squares regression (OLSR), multidimensional regression spline (MARS) and, of course, linear regression.

There are also regression variants that are used in machine learning, such as ridge regression. It is also known as weight loss. It is also known as the Tikhon-Miller method and the Phillips-Twomey method. Variants try to simplify models to reduce the complexity of the system that provides better support for generalization.

Steps in developing a machine learning application

Our approach to understanding and developing an application using machine learning in this book will follow a procedure similar to the following:

1. **Data Collection**: You can collect samples by scraping a website and extracting data, or you can get information from an RSS feed or an API. You could have a device collect measurements of wind speed and send them to you, or blood glucose levels, or anything that can be measured. The number of options is endless. To save time and effort, you can use publicly available data.

2. **Prepare the input data**. Once you have these data, you must ensure that it is in a usable format. The format to use is the Python list. The advantage of having this standard format is that you can mix and match algorithms and data sources. You may have to do some specific algorithm format here. Some algorithms need features in a special format, some algorithms can deal with objective variables and features like strings, and some of them have to be integers. The specific format algorithm is trivial in comparison to data collection

3. **Analyze the input data**. This is looking at the data from the previous task. This could be as simple as seeing the

data you have parsed in a text editor to make sure that steps 1 and 2 are working and do not have a lot of empty values. You can also see the data to see if it can recognize any pattern or if there is something obvious, like some data points that are very different from the rest of the set. Tracing data in one, two or three dimensions can also help. But most of the time you will have more than three features and you cannot easily plot the data through all the functions at once. You could, however, use some advanced to distil multiple dimensions to two or three so that you can visualize the data.

4. **If you are working with a production system and you know what the data should be like, or trust its source, you can skip this step**. This step requires human involvement, and for an machine system, one does not want human involvement. The value of this step is that it makes you understand that you do not have junk coming in.

5. **Train the algorithm.** This is where learning the machine takes place. This step and the next step are where the "core" algorithms are found, depending on the algorithm. It feeds the algorithm good clean data of the first two steps and extracts knowledge or information. This knowledge is often stored in a format that is easily usable by a machine for the next two steps. In the case of unsupervised learning, there is no training step because it has no objective value. Everything is used in the next step.

6. **Test the algorithm**. This is where the information learned in the previous step is put into use. When you are evaluating an algorithm, you will test it to see how well it does. In the case of supervised learning, you have some

known values that you can use to evaluate the algorithm. In unsupervised learning, you may have to use other metrics to evaluate success. In any case, if you are not satisfied,

You can go back to step 4, change some things and try again. Often the collection or preparation of the data may have been the problem, and you will have to go back to step 1.

7. **Use it**. Here you make a real program to do some homework, and once again you see if all the previous steps worked as you hoped. You may find some new data and have to review steps 1-5. We will now talk about a language for implementing machine learning applications: We need understandable language for a wide range of people. We also need a language that has libraries written for a series of tasks, especially matrix mathematics. We would also like to have a language with an active developer community. Python is the best option for these reasons.

How to build Ensemble Models in machine learning? (with code in R)

What is ensembling?

In general, ensembling is a technique of combining two or more algorithms of similar or dissimilar types called base learners. This is done to make a more robust system that incorporates the predictions of all base learners. It can be understood as conference room meeting between multiple operators to make a decision on whether the price of an action is going to rise or not.

Since they all have a different understanding of the stock market and therefore a different mapping function of the problem statement for the desired result. Therefore, you are supposed to make varied predictions about stock price based on your understanding of the market.

Now we can take all these predictions into account when making the final decision. This will make our final decision more robust, accurate and less prone to bias. The final decision would have been opposed if one of these traders had taken this decision alone.

You can consider another example of a candidate through multiple rounds of job interviews. The final decision on the candidate's ability is usually made based on the feedback from all the interviewers. Although a single interviewer might not be able to test the candidate for each required skill and trait. But the combined feedback from multiple interviewers helps in a better evaluation of the candidate.

Some of the basics that you should keep in mind before going into more detail are:

- **Average**: Defined as taking the average of the predictions of the models in case of regression problem or in predicting the probabilities for the classification problem.
- **Voting majority**: It is defined as taking the prediction with the maximum votes / recommendation of multiple model predictions while predicting the results of a classification problem.

Weighted average: In this case, different weights are applied to the predictions of several models, then taking the average, which means giving a high or low importance to the result of the specific model.

In practical terms, there may be some **ways in which different models can be assembled**. But these are some of the techniques that are most used:

1. **Bagging**: Bagging is also known as boot aggregation. To understand the bagging, we must first understand the boot. Bootstrapping is a sampling technique in which we choose 'n' observations or rows outside the original data set of 'n' rows as well. But the key is that each row is selected with the replacement of the original dataset so that each row is equally likely to be selected at each iteration. Let's say we have three rows numbered 1, 2 and 3.
Therefore, we can have multiple bootstrap samples of the same data. Once we have these multiple bootstrap samples, we can grow trees for each of these bootstrap samples and use the majority vote or average concepts to get the final prediction. This is how bagging works. One important thing to note here is that it is done primarily to reduce variance. Now the random forest uses this concept but goes one step further to further reduce the variance by randomly choosing a subset of features as well for each bootstrapped sample to make the divisions during training.

2. **Boosting**: Boosting is a sequential technique in which the first algorithm is trained on the entire data set and the later algorithms are constructed by adjusting the residuals of the first algorithm, thus giving greater

weight to those observations that were poorly predicted by the previous model.

It is based on creating a series of weak students, each of which may not be good for the whole data set, but is good for some part of the data set. Therefore, each model increases the performance of the set.

It is very important to keep in mind that boosting focuses on reducing bias. This makes the impulse algorithms prone to excessive tuning. Therefore, tuning parameters becomes a crucial part of the boost algorithms to prevent them from overfeeding. Some examples of boost are XGBoost, GBM, AdaBoost, etc..

3. **Stacking**: In multi-layer stacking machine learning models are placed one over another where each of the models passes their predictions to the model in the upper layer, and the top layer model makes decisions based on the outputs of the models layered down.

Here, we have two **layers of machine learning models**:

- **Lower layer models** (d1, d2, d3) that receive the original input characteristics (x) of the data set.
- **Top layer model**, f which takes the output of the lower layer models (d1, d2, d3) as its input and predicts the final output.
- A key thing to keep in mind here is that bending predictions are used while predicted for training data.

Here, we have used only two layers, but can be any number of layers and any number of models in each layer. Two of the **key principles for selecting models**:

- Individual models meet specific precision criteria.
- Model predictions of several individual models are not highly correlated with predictions from other models.

One thing you may have realized is that we have used the top layer model that takes as input the predictions from the lower layer models. This top layer model can also be replaced by many other simpler formulas like:

- Average
- Majority vote
- Average weight

Advantages and disadvantages of ensembling

Advantages

- Ensembling is a proven method to improve the accuracy of the model and works in most cases.
- It is the key ingredient to win almost all hackathons of machine learning.
- Assembly makes the model more robust and stable, ensuring decent performance in test cases in most scenarios.
- You can use ensembling to capture complex linear and simple as well as non-linear relationships in the data. This can be done using two different models and form a set of two.

Disadvantages

Ensembling reduces the interpretability of the model and makes it very difficult to get any crucial idea of the business in the end.

It is time-consuming and therefore may not be the best idea for real-time applications.

Selecting models to create a set is an art that is difficult to master.

What is Bagging, Boosting and Stacking?

Let's look at each of these individually and try to understand the differences between these terms:

Bootstrap Aggregating is a set method. First, we create random samples of the training data set (sub-sets of training data set). Then we build a classifier for each sample. Finally, the results of these multiple classifiers are combined using average or majority voting. Bagging helps reduce variance.

Boosting provides sequential learning of predictors. The first predictor is learned throughout the dataset, while the following are learned in the training set based on the previous performance. Begin by classifying the original data set and giving equal weights to each observation. If classes are predicted incorrectly using the first student, then it gives greater weight to the lost classified observation. Being an iterative process, it continues to add classifier apprentice until a limit is reached on the number of models or precision. Impulse has shown better predictive accuracy than bagging, but also tends to over-adjust to training data as well. The most common example of boosting is AdaBoost and Gradient Boosting. You can also check out these articles to know more about boosting algorithms.

Stacking works in two phases. First, we used several base classifiers to predict the class. Second, a new student is used to combine his predictions with the aim of reducing the generalization error.

Can we ensemble multiple models of same ML algorithm?

Yes, we can combine multiple models of the same ML algorithms, but combining multiple predictions generated by different algorithms would normally give better predictions. It is due to diversification or independent nature compared to others. For example, random forest predictions, a KNN and a Naive Bayes can be combined to create a stronger final prediction set compared to the combination of three random forest models. The key to creating a powerful set is the diversity of models. A set with two techniques that are very similar will work poorly than a more diverse set of models.

Example: Let's say we have three models (A, B and C). A B and C have prediction accuracy of 85%, 80%, and 55% respectively. But A and B are found to be highly correlated whereas C is a thin correlation with A and B. Should we combine A and B? No, we should not, because these models are highly correlated. Therefore, we will not combine these two as this set will not help reduce any generalization error. It is advisable to combine A & C or B & C.

How can we identify the weights of the different set models?

One of the most common challenges with cluster modeling is to find optimal weights to assemble base models. In general, we assume equal weight for all models and take the average of the predictions. But is this the best way to deal with this challenge?

There are several methods for finding the optimum weight to match all core students. These methods provide a fair understanding about finding the right weight. Here is a list of some of the methods below:

- Find collinearity among base students, then identify base models to assemble. After that, look at the cross-validation score (scoring ratio) of the identified base models to find the weight.
- Find the algorithm to return the optimal weight for the basic apprentices. We can also solve the same problem using methods like:

Forward Selection of students

Selection with replacement

The bagging of ensembled methods

You can also look at the winning solution of Kaggle competitions / data science to understand other methods to deal with this challenge

The two major benefits of Ensemble models:

- **Better prediction**
- **More stable model**

The aggregate opinion of multiple models is less noisy than other models. In finance, It is called "Diversification" a mixed portfolio of many stocks will be much less variable than just one of the stocks alone. This is also why your models will be better with an ensemble of models rather than the individual. One of the cautions with ensemble models is over fitting although bagging takes care of it largely.

In today's competitive world, every organization tries to outsmart its competitors to gain market share and improve the bottom line. They are constantly looking for new strategies and techniques to achieve this objective.

 Machine learning is the new buzz word that has caught the attention of the organizations. Machine learning is a type of artificial intelligence that is related to the patterns and study of certain systems that use the huge input of data for its working.

Here are the four things about this naive technique.

Complex pattern recognition - It has one of the most important features that it can be used to study and understand complex patterns in the data. It helps to give meaning to the data by providing a relationship and quantifying the same. This feature eliminates irrelevant data from the huge chunk of data and you are left with pure relevant data that can be used to dig out various useful insights. It also helps the user to understand primary and secondary variables for a set of information. This helps in the pre-processing technique and acceleration process.

Ability to take intelligent decisions - The process can take decisions with or without the guidance of a user. It is a type of artificial intelligence which makes decisions based on the input and the desired output. It selects the best optimum choice from a given set of options which will benefit the user as compared to the other

Self-Improving and Modifying: Suppose you teach in a Math class, who will you prefer as a student; a kid who makes the same mistake again and again or a kid who corrects his last mistake and improves next time? Your answer will more likely be the later one as it reduces your efforts by a great deal. Same is the case here. It has the characteristic of improving the standards of its decision-making ability and modifies itself for better; enhanced outputs benefit the user to a greater extent. It refines itself with multiple iterations on a particular problem and provides the user with an optimum solution.

Adds power to your analytics; Machine learning enhances the power of analytics. Consumer behavior is dynamic and changes constantly. It is important to tap and respond to these changes. It optimizes complex goals and improves lifetime value of the customers. It helps in building new predictive models to nullify the change. Another important characteristic is that it helps to track the process of a particular campaign right from the start of the campaign and not wait till the campaign ends.

CHAPTER FOUR

How to choose the right algorithm

With all the different algorithms, how can you choose which one to use? First, you need to consider your goal. What are you trying to get out of this? (Do you want a probability that it might rain tomorrow, or do you want to find groups of voters with similar interests?) Those are the big questions. Let's talk about your goal. If you're trying to predict or forecast a target value, then you need to look into supervised learning. If not, then unsupervised learning is the place you want to be. If you've chosen supervised learning, what's your target value? Is it a discrete value like Yes/No, 1/2/3, A/B/C, or Red/Yellow/Black? If so, then you want to look into classification. If the target value can take on a number of values, say any value from 0.00 to 100.00, or -999 to 999, or + to -, then you need to look into regression.

If you're not trying to predict a target value, then you need to look into unsupervised learning. Are you trying to fit your data into some discrete groups? If so and that's all you need, you should look into clustering. Do you need to have some numerical estimate of how strong the fit is into each group? If you answer yes, then you probably should look into a density estimation algorithm.

The second thing you need to consider is your data. You should spend some time getting to know your data, and the more you know about it, the better you'll be able to build a successful application. Things to know about your data are these: Are the features nominal or continuous? Are there missing values in the features? If there are missing values, why are there missing values? Are there outliers in the data? Are you looking for a needle in a haystack, something that happens very infrequently? All of these features about your data can help you narrow the algorithm selection process. With the algorithm narrowed, there's no single answer to what the best algorithm is or what will give you the best results. You're going to have to try different algorithms and see how they perform.

There are other machine learning techniques that you can use to improve the performance of a machine learning algorithm. The relative performance of two algorithms may change after you process the input data. Finding the best algorithm is an iterative process of trial and error. Many of the algorithms are different, but there are some common steps you need to take with all of these algorithms when building a machine learning application.

What Python has that other languages don't have

There are high-level languages that allow you to do matrix math such as MATLAB and Mathematica. MATLAB has some built-in features that make machine learning easier. MATLAB is also very fast. The problem with MATLAB is that to legally use it will cost you a few thousand dollars. There are third-party add-ons to MATLAB but nothing on the scale of an open source project. There are matrix math libraries for low-level languages such as Java and C. The problem with these languages is that it takes a lot of code to get simple things done. First, you have to typecast variables, and then with Java, it seems that you have to write setters and getters every time you sneeze. Don't forget sub classing. You have to subclass methods even if you aren't going to use them. At the end of the day, you have written a lot of code—sometimes tedious code—to do simple things. This isn't the case with Python. Python is clear, concise, and easy to read. Python is easy for nonprogrammers to pick up. Java and C aren't so easy to pick up and much less concise than Python

Sensors and the data deluge

We have a tremendous amount of human-created data from the World Wide Web, but recently more nonhuman sources of data have been coming online. The technology behind the sensors isn't new, but connecting them to the web is new. It's estimated that shortly after this book's publication physical sensors will create 20 percent of no video internet traffic.

1. The following is an example of an abundance of free data, a worthy cause, and the need to sort through the data. In 1989, the Loma Prieta earthquake struck northern California, killing 63 people, injuring 3,757, and leaving thousands homeless. A similarly sized earthquake struck Haiti in 2010, killing more than 230,000 people. Shortly after the Loma Prieta earthquake, a study was published using low-frequency magnetic field measurements claiming to foretell the earthquake.

2. A number of subsequent studies showed that the original study was flawed for various reasons.

3,4 Suppose we want to redo this study and keep searching for ways to predict earthquakes so we can avoid the horrific consequences and have a better understanding of our planet. What would be the best way to go about this study? We could buy magnetometers with our own money and buy pieces of land to place them on. We could ask the government to help us out and give us money and land on which to place these magnetometers. Who's going to make sure there's no tampering with the magnetometers, and how can we get readings from them? There exists another low-cost solution. Mobile phones or smartphones today ship with three axis magnetometers. The smartphones also come with operating systems where you can execute your own programs; with a few lines of code you can get readings from the magnetometers hundreds of times a second. Also, the phone already has its own communication system set up; if you can convince people to install and run your program, you could record a large amount of magnetometer data with very little investment. In addition to the magnetometers, smartphones carry a large number of other sensors including yaw rate gyros, three-axis accelerometers, temperature sensors, and GPS receivers, all of which you could use to support your primary measurements.

How large is your training set?

If your training set is small, high bias / low variance classifiers (e.g., Bayes Naive) have an advantage over low/high variance classifiers (e.g., KNN), since the latter will overlap. But low-variance / high-variance classifiers begin to gain as their training set grows (they have a smaller asymptotic error) since high-bias classifiers are not powerful enough to provide accurate models.

You can also think of this as a generative model versus discriminatory model distinction.

Advantages of some particular algorithms

Advantages of Naive Bayes: Super simple, you're only doing a lot of beads. If the NB conditional independence hypothesis is indeed fulfilled, a Bayes Naive classifier will converge faster than discriminative models such as logistic regression, so it needs less training data. And even if the assumption of NB is not met, an NB classifier still often does a great job in practice. A good bet if you want something quick and easy that works quite well.

Its main disadvantage is that you can not learn the interactions between features (for example, you can not learn that even though you love movies with Brad Pitt and Tom Cruise, you hate movies where they are together).

Advantages of Logistic Regression: There are many ways to regularize your model, and you do not have to worry as much about the correlating features as you do on Naive Bayes. You also have a nice probabilistic interpretation, unlike decision trees or SVMs, and you can easily upgrade your model to take on new data (using a gradient descent method online), again unlike decision trees or SVMs. Use it if you want a probabilistic framework (e.g., to easily adjust classification thresholds, to say when you are not sure, or to obtain confidence intervals) or if you expect to receive more training data in the future that you want to quickly incorporate into your model.

Advantages of Decision Trees: Easy to interpret and explain. They easily handle feature interactions and are not parametric, so you do not have to worry about outliers or whether the data are linearly separable (for example, decision trees easily handle instances where you have class A in the Lower end of some characteristic x, class B in the middle range of the characteristic x, and an again in the upper end).

 A disadvantage is that they are not compatible with online learning, so you have to rebuild your tree when new examples come up.

Another disadvantage is that they overlap easily, but that's where the set methods like random forests (or power trees) come in. In addition, random forests are often the winner of many problems in sorting (usually slightly by In front of SVMs) are fast and scalable, and you do not have to worry about fine tuning a lot of parameters like it does with SVM, so they seem to be very popular these days.

Advantages of SVMs: High accuracy, nice theoretical guarantees over overfitting, and with an appropriate kernel can work well even if you are data is not linearly separable in the low feature space. Especially popular in text classification problems where large dimension spaces are the norm. Memory intensive, difficult to interpret, and kind of annoying to run and tune, however, so I think the random forests are starting to steal the crown.

CHAPTER FIVE

How Machine Learning Will Impact Event Management

Forward-thinking companies have their eyes on machine learning. Google has long emphasized its priorities in the pursuit of machine learning and artificial intelligence. Of course, they are not the only ones. Recent Twitter acquisition of Magic Pony Technology indicates its keen interest in learning machines as well.

Apart from being news and a buzz word, machine learning and its developments have big implications for the businesses and the society in general. Specifically for the event industry, what can we expect regarding how machine learning will impact events?

In this book, we will explore current machine learning applications and make thoughtful predictions of how machine learning can be applied to event management. But first, let's set some key definitions.

What is the difference: Learning Machine, A.I. and beyond

In machine learning, the computer can automatically improve through experience. In that sense; it's self-learning. Based on data that is fed or collected by the computer, the computer is able to make new decisions for itself to improve efficiency and achieve its goals.

It is part of the broad umbrella of A.I. Or artificial intelligence, the quest to design computers that mimic but exceed human capacities, and provide practical solutions to real-world problems.

Data mining, another buzz word, is the process of collecting and understanding large amounts of digital information. Because computers act on information, data mining is the basis for A.I. and machine learning.

Algorithms are problem-solving formulas. They are the rules or directives that a computer follows when processing information and completing operations.

Deep learning, one more concept of trends, takes the machine learning to the next level. In deep learning, the machine is designed to function as human neural networks and be capable of higher level skills, such as understanding language and recognizing objects.

The above concepts are interrelated. In the media, these terms are widely defined and sometimes used interchangeably. To distil these concepts into an essence, we can say that computers are becoming more intelligent and capable. The implication is that we can take advantage of all this for greater productivity.

Current Practical Applications of Machine Learning

Machine learning is often used to digest and analyze large volumes of information, which humans can not process quickly and efficiently by themselves.

Some of the most common machine learning applications includes:

Netflix and Amazon recommendations that "learn" your preferences

Web search results that fit your viewing history and demographics

Real-time web and mobile ads that "look" to be relevant to you

Email spam filtering

Analysis of the feeling based on text

Prediction of equipment failure

Forecast of demand

Price optimization

Fraud detection

Recognition of images and patterns

Auto-driving cars

Robotics

As you can see, we use machine learning in many industries, and it is already part of our daily lives. When it comes to event planning, we can say that machine learning already has some peripheral applications. For example, it affects the ranking of the pages of our event in the search results. But we want to imagine the future of machine learning in this industry. Based on current machine learning applications, we can predict future uses and benefits for the event industry.

How Machine Learning Can Benefit Event Management

1. Inform your planning and decision making

One of the most popular applications of machine learning now is for prediction and decision making. Computers can read and analyze much more information than human minds can. Relying on the calculation for decision-making gives companies a greater competitive advantage.

Let's take professional sports, for example, and the analysis company Second Spectrum. The second Spectrum collects and analyses performance data from athletes and uses this data to help coaches and teams win. Half of the NBA teams now rely on Second Spectrum software to administer and train teams.

In addition to strategizing in sports, machine learning can help make recruitment and recruitment decisions. In a McKinsey & Company experiment, three algorithms were used to predict which candidates from a group of 10,000 applicants were most suitable for a particular company. Calculus forecasts closely matched real-world recruitment results, demonstrating the effectiveness of machine learning to analyze curriculum data and make reliable recommendations.

In addition, in the above experiment, the computer selected a slightly larger number of applicants than real-world hiring managers, suggesting that machine learning can help us overcome preconceptions and make unbiased decisions.

Brian Uzzi, a professor at Kellogg School of Management, echoes this idea when he says, "Through the man-machine associations, leaders will be able to strip away latent biases and make more empirical decisions, which will lead to more Creative and intuitive. "

Regarding event management, machine learning can help in the selection of experts and speakers. Using the learning machine for the speaker selection process could help some industries and events to overcome a trend towards panels only for men. It can also save event planners large amounts of time by comparing speaker ratings and work histories if they could rely on data analysis software.

Similarly, learning the machine could be used in the local hunting process. Just as Netflix suggests relevant movies and Amazon finds suitable products, a venue search platform could help event planners find the right venue for their event and suggest several appropriate options based on the organizers' story and preferences.

2. Allow you to make faster, more accurate decisions

Hotel managers are already using machine learning to help with a key aspect of their business: price optimization. Algorithms can determine the optimum room price at any given time by analyzing supply and demand in real time and looking at the competition of surrounding hotels, holiday homes, and related accommodation types. Calculations that take hours for humans to compute (after which, the results would be obsolete), an algorithm can determine in real time and adjust prices automatically.

Beyond this, hotels know that different types of customers are willing to pay different prices for the same room. Therefore, algorithms are used to predict the cost that a highly satisfied customer would be willing to pay for a return visit, compared to the cost that a price sensitive customer would be willing to pay. In this way, price optimization is achieved not only by reflecting current supply, demand, and competition but also optimized for the individual buyer, based on buyer's purchase history and buying behavior.

The type of price optimization currently used in hotel management could also be transferred to event management. Large events often have different price levels and a variety of programs and hosting packages. They offer principles of bird prices, flash sales, group prices and various promotions. How can event managers know the optimal price to set each type of ticket? What is the best term for an early sale or flash sale? Algorithms can help decide these details, and predict when there will be an avalanche of buyers (time to withhold on rebates) or when there will be a pause in sales (time to take in the push of marketing). This type of predictive analysis can optimize the profitability of the events, as well as optimize the revenue of the hotels.

3. Predict the feelings and preference of the attendees

The prediction of feeling is another popular application of machine learning. Also called opinion mining, sentiment analysis helps organizations determine public opinion about a particular product or topic, based on text analysis, usually web reviews, social networking messages and online conversations. The Obama administration, for example, used sentiment analysis to determine public opinion toward policy announcements during the 2012 elections.

In summary, the feeling analysis tells you how your audience feels, what they like or do not like. In this way, feeling analysis is useful for event organizers who want to know which artists to book for next year, what speakers to invite and what themes to choose for a future conference. Will your future conference participants want to know about AI applications or UX design? How popular and shocking were the talks and workshops last year, and which ones should they repeat or improve? Feeling analysis can help event planners get information on areas like these, giving planners a predictive wisdom for future events.

In addition to analyzing the feeling, the machine learning can also satisfy the preferences of the attendees. The music platform Spotify, for example, can adapt to the musical preferences of the listeners and suggest appropriate clues. One day, an event sourcing platform can achieve the same level of customization. Algorithms could be used to suggest workshops and seminars relevant to conference attendees, helping to reduce attendee time in navigation and event research. Attendees of the event could be alerted of upcoming concerts in their area for bands and musical genres that match their tastes. Event merchandise and conference resources could be suggested purchases, and add-ons automatically offered to visitors to the event page as well.

4. Curate and categorize conference content

Learning the machine allows us to cure, label and categorize large amounts of content. This content library can be accessed by viewers looking for information on various topics, and algorithms can help viewers find what they are looking for.

It's exactly what YouTube has been doing; using algorithms to suggest related content and helping viewers find the most relevant query results. YouTube algorithms mimic Google's deep learning algorithms used for search recommendations. Vice President of YouTube Product Management Johanna Wright tells TechCrunch: "We want YouTube to communicate this feeling that it understands it."

This artificial feeling of understanding and personalization achieved through machine learning can be transferred to event management. For organizers who have a history of running a large number of events, imagine if all of your previous workshop, seminar, and presentation content were cured and labelled. Attendees paid members or subscribers could access this content library, where they could receive help from recommendation algorithms by discovering interesting playlists and relevant content.

5. Achieve greater customer segmentation

The data allows us to discover more about our customers, giving us a better understanding of the best way to connect with them. In one famous case, retailer Target discovered that one of her clients was pregnant even before her own family knew about it. Based on what Target had analysed about this customer's purchase history, the company proactively shipped pregnancy coupons and baby products in the hope of winning it as a lifetime customer. Her family was greatly surprised to report it to the store.

Apart from extreme cases, data anal analysis can help companies and event planners get new customers. For example, you may be able to segment who in your mailing list is new to your industry and interested in career development events, or who is based in New York and possibly can attend your next conference. A potential customer would be categorized and put into a relevant marketing campaign without any intervention from you or a team member, saving you time and resources.

6. Take the opportunity to come A.I. Trends in service and hospitality

In a strange example of machine learning applied to the hospitality industry, the Japanese hotel Henn na is made up of robots. Upon entering, guests are greeted by three multilingual machines: a humanoid woman, a dinosaur robot, and a futuristic robot. A robotic arm sits in the lobby and places guests' belongings in wardrobes for custody - a robotic wardrobe.

The founder of the hotel, Hideo Sawada, created Henn na to save labor costs and highlight A.I. innovation. Sawada says: "In the future, we would like to have over 90 percent of hotel-operated robot services."

How Edge Computing and Serverless Deliver Scalable Machine Learning Services

Learning, Edge Computing and Serverless are the three key technologies that will redefine Cloud Computing platforms.

Machine Learning (ML) is becoming an integral part of modern applications. From the web to the mobile to IoT, ML is driving the next generation of applications through user experiences and embedded intelligence.

After virtualization and contention, Serverless is emerging as the next wave of computing services. Serverless or Service-like (FaaS) attempts to simplify the developer experience by minimizing the operational overhead of code deployment and management. Contemporary applications designed as micro services are built on FaaS platforms such as AWS Lambda, Azure Functions, Google Cloud Functions and Open Whisk.

Edge Computing takes the calculation closer to the applications. Each edge location simulates the public cloud by exposing a compatible set of services and endpoints that applications can consume. Everything is ready to redefine the business infrastructure.

These three emerging technologies - Serverless, Edge Computing and Machine Learning - will be the main technological drivers for the next generation of infrastructure. The goal of this book is to explain how developers will benefit from the combination of these technologies.

Data availability, ample storage capacity, and sufficient computing power are essential to implement Machine Learning. Cloud becomes the natural setting for dealing with Machine Learning. Data Scientists are relying on the cloud to ingest and store massive data sets. They are also using the payment infrastructure as they process and analyze the data. With cheaper storage and advanced computing platforms powered by GPUs and FPGAs, the cloud is fast becoming the destination for building complex ML models.

Machine Learning Trends that will define 2017

 Learning machine has been silently working in the background for years, driving mobile applications and search engines. But recently it has become a more popular buzzword, with virtually all recent technological advances involving some aspect of machine learning. An impressive increase in data and computing capabilities has made this exponential progress possible.

The remarkable growth of sophistication and machine learning applications will define the technological trends of 2017. Their effects will depend on whether the application adds value and benefits to society as a whole and whether it has the potential to solve real-world problems. These are the five major trends that will define machine learning in 2017.

1. Machine learning in finance

The financial sector has historically used machine learning in consumer services, such as credit verification and fraud investigation. However, recently, with more accessible computing power and open source tools, the financial sector uses machine learning in applications ranging from loan approval and risk assessment to asset management.

A recent breakthrough called sentiment analysis involves considering the impact of social media trends and news on commodity prices. Machine learning is used to replicate the human response to current issues for decision-making in hedge fund trading. Dr. Ben Goertzel of the Open Cog Foundation said that what is missing in current AI is "cognitive energy" that integrates physiological and biochemical processes into an amalgam of interconnections and associations, resulting in human intelligence. The foundation has made some progress in bringing this component to AI. The hedge fund is fully traded independent of human interaction and uses probabilistic logic to analyze and interpret daily market data, news and social media, make predictions and decide the best course of action.

This application will definitely add value to market sectors and transform the way the economy is traded. It takes into consideration influential factors in the markets, such as trend news, thus making predictions that humans do not have the ability to.

2. Autonomous driving

With a car fatality rate of 1.2 million people a year and 90 percent attributed to human error, the idea of autonomous vehicles has undeniable merit. AVs comprise a variety of sensors to evaluate distance, speed, and terrain. Consequently, vehicles are more equipped to deal with an emergency than their human counterparts.

To illustrate the potential, imagine this scenario: An AV stands in a red light in danger of impact from behind by a rapidly approaching car. The AV suddenly accelerates at the intersection to avoid a collision and simultaneously changes the lights to red. The motivation for this type of technology is to preserve life and having fleets of AVs on the streets will exclude human error, road rage, and other dynamic traffic problems.

3. Exploration of space

In the field of space exploration, autonomous driving is not a new concept. AutoNav has been driving the Mars rover since 2004. The radiation and reliability problems that have kept space computing on the back foot are being relieved. Research on improving the reliability of the Mars Rover is under way, with learning the machine at its core. Through the use of a "vision-based terrain classifier and a risk-conscious path planner," it aims to impart a similar human-risk thinking to the rover, allowing for a safer ride.

Being able to navigate remotely with more precision will allow exploration of extreme environments. For example, subsurface ocean research in Europe is now a different possibility.

4. Health and medicine

Precision medicine challenges the traditional broad spectrum approach. This new form of health care involves constant biometric data transmitted by wearables, algorithms and molecular tools.

This development is changing medicine, allowing non-subjective identification of symptoms and offering platforms to interpret and connect data from the Week Ebook. The success of this system depends on the development of accurate and consistent machine learning tools to decide the best treatment regime based on data collected specifically to the individual.

This overcomes cultural and linguistic barriers and therefore has an inherent value for the medical profession and can also mitigate the emotional responses of human physicians that often detract from accurate diagnoses and treatment protocols.

5. Humanitarian aid

Drones are the logical solution to getting supplies remote and dangerous places. This is especially true for large distances locations from the control center. Qualcomm unveiled a drone platform that uses flight control and machine learning. Machine learning is not a new concept in drone technology, but what makes this particular version superior is that the drone can actively learn about the environments it occupies without prior knowledge. The autonomous flight will be valuable for humanitarian aid services.

Learning the machine is the core of many innovations that are set to improve our everyday lives. In 2017, they will also have a discernible positive consequence for society and the

Economy

How to Implement a Machine Learning Algorithm

Benefits of Implementing Machine Learning Algorithms

Practical Skills

It is developing valuable skills when it implements hand-learning algorithms. Skills such as mastery of the algorithm, skills that can aid in the development of production systems and skills that can be used for classical research in the field

Three examples of skills you can develop are listed:

Domain: The implementation of an algorithm is the first step towards the domain of the algorithm. You are forced to understand the algorithm intimately when it is implemented. It is also creating its laboratory for a special action to help internalize the calculation is done over time, such as by debugging and adding measures to evaluate the running process.

Production Systems: Custom implementations of algorithms are normally required for production systems because of the changes that need to be made to the algorithm for reasons of efficiency and effectiveness. Better, faster, less resource intensive results can ultimately lead to lower costs and higher revenue in business, and application algorithms per part help develop the skills to deliver these solutions.

Review of the literature: When implementing an algorithm that is carrying out the research. It is forced to locate and read several canonical and formal descriptions of the algorithm. It is also likely to look for and review other algorithm implementations to confirm their understanding. It is conducting specific research and learning to read and make practical use of research publications.

Process

There is a process you can follow to accelerate your ability to learn and implement a machine learning algorithm by hand from scratch. The more algorithms you implement, the faster and more efficient you will get and the more you will develop and customize your process. You can use the process described below.

1. Select the programming language: Select the programming language you want to use for the implementation. This decision can influence the standard APIs and libraries that you can use in your implementation.
2. Select Algorithm: Select the algorithm you want to implement from scratch. Be as specific as possible. This means not only the type and type of algorithm but also go as far as selecting a specific description or implementation that you want to implement.
3. Select Problem: Select a canonical problem or set of problems that you can use to test and validate the implementation of the algorithm. Machine learning algorithms do not exist in isolation.
4. Research Algorithm: Locate documents, books, websites, libraries and any other description of the algorithm you can read and learn. Although ideally, you want to have a key description of the algorithm from which to work, you will want to have multiple perspectives on the algorithm. This is useful because multiple perspectives will help you internalize the algorithm description faster and overcome the obstacles of any ambiguity or assumptions made in the

description (there are always ambiguities in algorithm descriptions).
5. Unit Test: Write unit tests for each function, even consider test driven development from the beginning of the project so that you are forced to understand the purpose and expectations of each unit of code before you implement them.

I strongly suggest porting algorithms from one language to another as a way of making rapid progress along this path, you can find plenty of open source implementations of algorithms that you can code review, diagram, internalize and re-implement in another language.

Consider open sourcing your code while you are developing it and after you have developed it. Comment it well and ensure it provides instructions on how to build and use it. The project will provide marketing for the skills you are developing and may just provide inspiration and help for someone else looking to make their start in machine learning. You may even be lucky enough to find a fellow programmer sufficiently interested to perform an audit or code review for you. Any feedback you get will be invaluable (even as motivation), actively seek it.

Extensions

Once you have implemented an algorithm, you can explore making improvements to the implementation. Some examples of improvements you could explore include:

- Experimentation: You can expose many of the micro-decisions you made in the algorithms implementation as parameters and perform studies on variations of those parameters. This can lead to new insights and disambiguation of algorithm implementations that you can share and promote.

- Optimization: You can explore opportunities to make the implementation more efficient by using tools, libraries, different languages, different data structures, patterns and internal algorithms. The knowledge you have of algorithms and data structures for classical computer science can be very beneficial for this type of work.
- Specialization: You may explore ways of making the algorithm more specific to a problem. This can be required when creating production systems and is a valuable skill. Making an algorithm more sproblems specific can also lead to increases in efficiency (such as running time) and efficacy (such as accuracy or other performance measures).
- Generalization: Opportunities can be created by making a specific algorithm more general. Programmers (like mathematicians) are uniquely skilled in abstraction, and you may be able to see how the algorithm could be applied to more general cases of a class of problem or other problems entirely.

Limitations

You can learn a lot by implementing machine learning algorithms by hand, but there are also some downsides to keep in mind.

- Redundancy: Many algorithms already have implementations, some very robust implementations that have been used by hundreds or thousands of researchers and practitioners around the world. Your implementation may be considered redundant, a duplication of effort already invested by the community.

- Bugs: New code that has few users is more likely to have bugs, even with a skilled programmer and unit tests. Using a standard library can reduce the likelihood of having bugs in the algorithm implementation.
- Non-intuitive Leaps: Some algorithms rely on non-intuitive jumps in reasoning or logic because of the sophisticated mathematics involved. It is feasible that an implementation that does not appreciate these leaps to be limited or even incorrect.

It is easy to comment on open source implementations of machine learning algorithms and raise many issues in a code review. It is much harder to appreciate the non-intuitive efficiencies that have been encoded in the implementation. This can be a trap in thinking.

You may find it beneficial to start with a slower intuitive implementation of a complex algorithm before considering how to change it to be programmatically less elegant, but computationally more efficient.

Example Projects

Some algorithms are easier to understand than others. In this post, I want to make some suggestions for intuitive algorithms from which you might like to select your first machine learning algorithm to implement from scratch.

- Ordinary Least Squares Linear Regression: Use two-dimensional data sets and model x from y. Print out the error for each iteration of the algorithm. Consider plotting the line of best fit and predictions for each iteration of the algorithm to see how the updates affect the model.

- k-Nearest Neighbor: Consider using two-dimensional data sets with two classes even ones that you create with graph paper so that you can plot them. Once you can plot and make predictions, you can plot the relationships created for each prediction decision the model makes.

- Perceptron: Considered the simplest artificial neural network model and very similar to a regression model. You can track and graph the performance of the model as it learns a dataset.

Summary

In this chapter, you learned the benefits of implementing machine learning algorithms by hand. You learned that you could understand an algorithm, make improvements and develop valuable skills by following this path.

You learned a simple process that you can follow and customize as you implement multiple algorithms from scratch and you learned three algorithms that you could choose as your first algorithm to implement from scratch.

CHAPTER SIX

The dawn of Machine learning in the enterprise

Companies are struggling to find value in the massive amounts of data they generate and save every day. Machine learning, the field of computational science centered on pattern recognition, is providing the necessary knowledge that brings greater understanding, predictive accuracy and prescriptive intelligence to corporate data sets, as well as contributing to various strategic results.

Machine apprenticeship applications play an increasing role in our daily lives. Whether it's Apple's Siri, Microsoft's Cortana machine wizards, pre-approved credit card offers, savings, and investment offerings from your bank, suggestions on Amazon, Expedia or Netflix, each is an example of learning in action. What everyone has in common is that each seeks to create the highest quality predictive intelligence in future behavior, based largely on historical data. In short, machine learning excels in solving more complex problems by creating accurate predictions without explicit computer programming.

The strategic role of Machine Learning in the company

Unlike advanced analytical techniques that seek causality in the first place, machine learning techniques are designed to look for opportunities to optimize decisions based on the predictive value of large-scale datasets. Data sets are composed of structured data, i.e., highly organized data, such as databases, and unstructured data, i.e., less organized data such as text in a sales contract or web traffic. The global proliferation of social networks is driving the growth of the latter type of data, making it increasingly important for companies to effectively take advantage of their unstructured data.

In business, machine learning is proving to be effective in the management of predictive and prescriptive tasks, allowing these companies to define which behaviors have the greatest propensity to drive the desired results. Companies are eager to compete and win more customers are applying machine learning to both the sales and marketing challenges.

Why adopting machine learning is accelerating in business

For business enterprises, machine learning can scale across a broad spectrum of business processes. Those that are directly related to the generation of income, often called cash quote, are among the most valuable applications and include sales, contract management, customer service, finance, legal, quality, prices, and fulfilment of orders.

The economy of cloud computing, cloud storage, the proliferation of sensors driving the Internet, and the widespread use of mobile devices that consume gigabytes of data in minutes are just a few of the many factors that accelerate the adoption of mobile learning. Machines today, add to this list the many challenges of creating a context within search engines, as well as the complex problems companies face in optimizing operations while predicting more likely outcomes, and the perfect environment is set for machine learning dramatically.

Where Machine Learning is Delivering Business Outcomes Today

The good news for companies is that all the data they have been saving for years can now become a competitive advantage and lead to the achievement of strategic objectives. Revenue and senior management teams are focusing on how they can leverage the core strengths of machine apprentices to transform the strategic vision of their business into reality. These teams focus first on business results and look for machine learning to accelerate and simplify, determining which factors influence purchase behavior more and lead to goals.

Sales, marketing, and channel management teams are using machine learning to optimize promotions, while compensation and discounts drive desired behavior through

Predicting the propensity to buy through channels, make personalized recommendations to customers, predict long-term customer loyalty, and anticipate potential revenue and credit risks for buyers are some specific applications of machine learning right now.

How Real Businesses Are Using Machine Learning

There is no doubt that learning the machine is at the top of the hype curve. And, of course, the reaction is already in full force: I heard that old joke "Machine learning is like teenage sex; everybody is talking about it, no one is doing it" about 20 times in the last week alone.

But from what I feel, running a company that allows a large number of real-world machine learning projects, it is clear that machine learning is already forcing massive changes in the running of companies.

There are just futuristic products like Siri and Amazon Echo. And it's not just the fact that companies normally think they have huge R & D budgets, like Google and Microsoft. I bet most Fortune 500 companies are already running more efficiently and making more money because of machine learning.

Make user-generated content valuable

The average part of the user generated content (UGC) is horrible. It's a lot worse than you think. It may be full of misspellings, vulgarity, or misinformation. But by identifying the best and worst UGC, machine learning models can filter out the bad and bubble up to the good without a real person to label each piece of content.

A similar thing happened some time ago with spam emails. Remember how bad spam was? Machine learning helped identify spam and eradicate it. These days, it is much rarer to see spam in your inbox every morning. Expect that to happen with UGC shortly.

Pinterest uses machine learning to show you more interesting content. Yelp uses machine learning to sort the photos that the user has uploaded. Next-door uses machine learning to sort the content on its message boards. Disqus uses machine learning to remove spam comments.

Finding products faster

As a search company, Google has always been at the forefront of hiring machine-learning researchers. In fact, Google recently put an expert on artificial intelligence in charge of the search. But the ability to index a huge database and get results that match a keyword has been around since the 1970s. What makes Google special is that it knows the most relevant result; the way you know it is through machine learning.

But Google does not just need smart search results. Home Depot needs to show what bathtubs in their huge inventory fit into someone's strange bathroom. Apple needs to show relevant applications in its app store. Intuit needs to display a good help page when a user types in a particular tax form.

Lyst's successful e-commerce start-ups to Trunk Archive employ machine learning to display high-quality content to its users. Other start-ups, such as Rich Relevance and Edge case employ machine learning strategies to give their business customers the benefits of machine learning when their users are searching for products.

Participate with clients

You may have noticed that the forms of "contact" have become thinner in recent years. That's another place where machine learning has helped streamline business processes. Instead of users self-selecting a problem and filling in endless form fields, auto-learning can examine the substance of an application and direct it to the right place.

That seems a small thing, but ticket labelling and routing can be a massive expense for large companies. Having a sales inquiry ends with the sales team or a complaint ending immediately at the tail of the customer service department saves companies a significant time and money all while ensuring that problems are prioritized and resolved as fast as possible.

Understand customer behavior

Machine learning also excels in the analysis of feeling. And while public opinion can sometimes seem soft to non-marketing people, it drives a lot of big decisions.

For example, let's say a movie studio puts a trailer for a summer box office hit. They can monitor social talk to see what is resonating with their target audience, and then adjust their ads to the surface immediately to what people are responding to. That puts people in theatres.

Another example: A game studio recently released a new title on a popular video game line without a game mode that fans expected. When the players took social networks to complain, the study was able to monitor and understand the conversation. The company ended up changing its launch schedule to add the feature, turning detractors into promoters.

How did they get weak signals from millions of tweets? They used machine learning. And in recent years, this kind of social media listening with machine learning has become standard operating procedure.

www.ingramcontent.com/pod-product-compliance
Lightning Source LLC
Chambersburg PA
CBHW070856070326
40690CB00009B/1875